Ode to an Egg

Author: John E. Potente

Artist: Arthur Ackermann

Published by Native America
www.nativeamerica.com
www.nativeamerica.org

First Printing 2018

All rights reserved. No portion of this book may be reproduced in any form or by any means, including electronic storage and retrieval systems, except by explicit, prior written permission of the publisher. except for brief passages excerpted for review or critical purposes.

Printed on Recycled paper
Acid-free for archival purposes.

ISBN: 978-0-9899136-1-4

Copyright 2015 by John Potente

Printed in the United States of America

Humpty Dumpty sat on a wall,
an egg that was wide and a little bit tall,
not quite so round, with a bulge in his middle,
and a shell that was lavish, but fragile and brittle.
His chest wore a coat, felted smartly in green,
his waist neatly belted, aquamarine.

His trunk was azure with splashes of white
and up on his crown was a cap of snow bright.
Humpty fared well, never one to lament,
surrounding himself with an air of content.
Choosing to welcome guests of all class,
he'd open his arms and greet as they'd pass.

Time honored Humpty, through dark and through light,
and gifted his shell with seasons and life.
Careful he minded his spot on the wall;
eight others beside him, befriending them all.
They circled around, all happy for Humpty,
though, unlike him, their shells were all empty.

One day a group of small travelers arrived
and asked of dear Humpty how would he mind
if up on his lap they could sit and then rest
to catch up on sleep and lay down their heads.
Humpty obliged, made home of his hips
and shared all the foods and fruits that were his.

Morning arrived, they woke one by one
and looked at the day with its new morning sun.
"What can we do to keep us amused?
Humpty's still sleeping and we're left to choose."
They climbed up his flanks to the top of his chin,
deciding between them where to begin.

Eyeing his coat of fresh garnish green,
one traveler held a small piece in between
his fingers and thought, "How nice it would be
to have some of this, all just for me."
And so he snipped a small part of some threads,
as he schemed to pretend it just fell off the end.

One who had seen the rip and its run
had scowled, "How thoughtless, this deed you have done.
But before he could finish his rave and his rant,
another had come and filled up his sack,
"If he could cut a small snip of the green,
why can't I dig for the gold that's beneath?"

A small inconvenience, Humpty had thought,
for hosting some travelers in need of a port.
Feeling the pinches and tugs on his shell,
he flinched and he winced, but had nothing to tell.
And so in his wish to accommodate all,
he abided in silence and pardoned their faults.

Leaders arose, no knowing how chosen;
a king, dukes and bishops and governers posing.
How happy was Humpty, to see them in gladness
and to think that they found a new home on his chest.
In the comforting circle of so many friends,
he smiled an ocean that spread to both ends.

Humpty Dumpty sighed as he grinned,
with an energy lit from his brow to his chin.
So proud of the marvelous green that he made,
where in havens of mountains and meadows it lay.
And now, on his belly, was a group he could woo
with wonders he worked and a beauty that bloomed.

Each day they toiled to take of his coat,
causing more missing threads and many more holes.
There were some who cautioned to leave him alone,
to simply enjoy the grace of his home.
Billions of years it took to assemble,
to disfigure the delicate fabric seamed sinful.

But the wary were few and were soon overridden
by others who reasoned in cant and in riddles.
The simple deeds of each day seemed offenseless
and were quickly condoned with their shallow pretenses.
On his face and his stomach, Humpty felt sore,
while not yet upset, was becoming unsure.

Night came along, again and again.
Each time it set down, there were much more of them.
So many travelers, one could not count
Fiefdoms emerged, all scattered about.
Crowding the acres many times over,
they became densely packed, shoulder to shoulder.

Kings looked over their fences to see
what other kings had and what could be seized.
And so their serfs were told as they toiled
that a fray would be needed to acquire more soil.
Upon Humpty's head, the battles began
with lances and fires for allegiance and land.

The king looked for ventures, justifying his rule,
to stuff his speeches and prop up approval,
while peasants groveled for recognition
from the king with his crown and their neighboring companions.
And so it was praise that became their incentive
to tout what they had and how they displayed it.

The issue of picking at Humpty's belongings
continued discord between right and wrongings.
Was there no limit to what they would trample
at Humpty's expense, with the green felt dismantled?
The king finally spoke and set a decree.
"It is lawful to take, but send some to me."

And so it was settled that this was allowed,
taking small bits, teasing threads out,
piling heaps in fierce competition,
not noticing how, soon all would be missing.
Some gathered for fun, and others for status,
until Humpty's coat was all pulled to tatters.

Smoke ascended and the air got hot,
Humpty warmed up and he melted on top.
The king convinced himself and his queen
that what they saw, they did not see.
It was better denying Humpty's dwindling health
than to forfeit their caper and give up their wealth.

Boredom returned to each of their minds.
Striving to please it, they claimed Humpty's sides.
Chipping away at his covetted shell,
they made trinkets and schillings, hoarding them well.
Some did it for power and others for pleasure.
Some wanted more, some knowing no better.

Years passed along, their tools got stronger,
the cracks they made deeper, the creases ran longer.
Humpty's green cloth had ripped apart
and the emerald patches were traded as lots.
"All is going just fine", the king swore,
"My sorcerer's brewing new food, air and water."

Humpty held on, hopeful and clement
but was sad that his name was seldomly mentioned.
The only time they hinted of him
was when he cried rain or tremored within.
With faith he looked to each generation,
that they might accept him and make him their friend.

Quarrels emerged over who held the most,
cutting and chipping his shell and his coat.
Torn and cracked, Humpty let out a moan,
but they shrugged and continued, business went on.
And as they bet over who would take all,
Humpty Dumpty had a great fall.

All the kings horses and all the kings men
tumbled, not knowing where they would end.
Down and around, they gasped as they struggled,
bumping peasants and princes and men in the middle.
Losing the lines that kept rich from poor,
all became frantic with stature no more.

"Due to him," one had fingered a reaper of threads,
"It was he who encouraged collecting, instead
of leaving the fabric of Humpty alone.
Disaster would never have broken our home."
He shook his finger from a fist tight together,
convinced that he solved the cause of this matter.

Voices were raised, accusing each other,
"It was you." "No, you, who started this clamor."
"I simply followed," came an innocent answer.
"Me too," many said, aloud and together.
And so some relinquished the blame from themselves,
absolving their souls from the cause they knew well.

One was still holding so tight to his cache
that his arms were locked stiff, but his legs would still thrash
in attempt to find some foothold or other,
but beneath was just air, no ground to recover.
Another let loose his chips from his mittens
and watched them disperse, one by one, in the distance.

Then rolling on down with their staves in between
were the almighty king and his jewel-haired queen.
Holding, above, his distinguishing crown,
he nodded to those he passed going down.
With arms at her sides to keep her robes folded,
the queen held her nose up, in perfect composure.

And so they descended from their chairs and their thrones,
the tillers, the merchants, and the unseated nobles.
Humpty had lost his fine fleece of green
and his ocean of blue and aquamarine.
Just as once, the king disavowed his wrongdoing
he now disbelieved he was losing his kingdom.

"Attention!" he railed at his men with their lances
"Raise up old Humpty to upright his stances."
His aide, who advised him, looked over with doubt,
"I think that dear Humpty is much too worn out."
"Then summon the masons to stir up the mortar.
Return all the pieces and put them in order."

The king continued commanding with fervor,
but his voice began cracking, you could hear his knees clatter.
In silent exit, the servants deserted
without words or contrition, and lack of direction.
The peasants had nothing left to possess,
and the king, now abandoned, nothing left to direct.

"Hurry," the queen said, in frenzied freefall,
"Let's ask of the others who visit the wall,
if they can oblige us better than he,
for Humpty's betrayed us, left us to flee.
There's eight more of them to give us a home.
I'm sure in no time we'll have a new throne."

So, the king and the queen climbed onto the ledge
of the trembling wall that surrendered its egg.
In haste, they aborted Humpty Dumpty,
and their traveling companions and their coffers now empty.
On top of the rampart that was no more than rubble
they looked to the heavens to plead with the others.

The almighty king went up to the first
and asked for a place where he and she just
might settle a while and gather their senses,
then he and the queen would live unpretentious.
"Surely, I'd help if I could in this way,
but my seat's boiling hot and would melt you away."

To the next, the king went and again he was told
that the plan would not work, this egg was too cold.
And the next shook its head in sad, sad regret
that his eggshell was covered with fumes head to neck.
The last of the eggs idled far at the edge
and was tilted too much to offer a bed.

One by one, the travelers disappeared in the black
of the empty, cold space with no sound coming back.
The threads and the chips of the shells floated on
till none were in sight, with every one gone.
Quiet had taken his place on the wall
with a seated depression where once sat the ball.

Humpty's companions witnessed his fate,
amd how his prize coat was divested in haste.
Alive with green-colored, petaled umbrellas
it ruffled with life through windows of rainbows.
For billions of years, he kept them in awe
He should have gone on, a few billion more.

The king and the queen bowed their heads
as the friends filed by and paid their respects.
How did the travelers not know then
what an honor it was to be hosted by him,
to live and be treated, for even a while,
on the most magnificent sphere of them all?

And so the king and the queen faced their fate,
realizing the earlier choices they made.
Perhaps if they'd left more of Humpty to be,
and found simple joy in their garden of Eden.
The queen humbly left a short note and it said
they couldn't put Humpty together again.

John Potente got his first scent of a garden in Queens, New York, when he was not yet a year old. At three years old, he watched blacktop being poured over shaved dirt to make a new street. At six, he learned the rhyme of Humpty Dumpty. When eleven, his father handed him a fledgling blue jay that fell from an oak tree. John raised the bird and watched it fly back up the tree. At eighteen years old, John climbed a water tower and saw how suburbia had grown beneath the forest of his home town. In college, he learned how life came about and how it spread on earth. After graduation, John filled up a backpack and hiked the Appalacian Trail through Virginia and Maryland, then the Grand Canyon, the Catskill Mountains, the foothills of the Sierra Nevada de Santa Marta and the moraines of Long Island. In adulthood, John earned a living fixing the dentition of members of his community. He also gave nature hikes, taught courses of the natural world, and edited the "Long Island Botanical Society". Later, serving on his county's environmental review board, he learned how decisions are made that affect the condition of the earth. His first published book detailed the ecology of salt marshes ("Tidal Marshes of Long Island, New York", published by the Torrey Botanical Society), and now sit on shelves of universities. "Ode to an Egg" is a siren, of sorts. It is meant to serve as call to humanity to listen to the Earth.

Arthur Ackermann had an early start helping the environment, by organizing a local clean up by his Cub Scout troupe in the first Earth Day. In childhood, he waded in golf course ponds looking for frogs and toads while getting cursed at by duffers. Growing up, Arthur admired Jacques Cousteau and was inspired to apply to the first high school devoted to marine science. Arthur went on to study under some of the kings of cartooning such as Harvey Kurtzman (the creator of Mad magazine), Will Eisner, Arnold Roth and Art Spiegelman (Pulitzer Prize winner). He learned from these great talents and idols, all under the same roof at the School of Visual Arts in Manhattan. Arthur's early work was included in a number of newspapers and shows, segueing into a successful career in magazine publication, working as part of an elite team of graphic professionals for Conde Nast (The New Yorker, Vanity fair, Vogue, Bon Appetit, and Glamour magazine). Arthur continues to keep a hand in environmental initiatives. He volunteers as part of a team that monitors horseshoe crabs on the beaches of Long Island, New York. Arthur is a believer in global warming and that attention and action to help the Earth is more important now, than ever. He became overly enthusiatic with this collaboration with his pencil sketches, water coloring and ultimately, refininement of the drawings with pen and ink. A small step using art for advocacy.